Designed by Flowerpot Press
www.FlowerpotPress.com
CHC-0909-0608
ISBN: 978-1-4867-2982-1
Made in China/Fabriqué en Chine

HOW DO METEOROLOGISTS PREDICT THE FUTURE?

A SCIENCE BOOK ABOUT METEOROLOGY

written by lisa spencer

illustrated by srimalie bassani

What is a meteorologist? Is it someone who studies meteors? No, but they do study things high up in the sky! A meteorologist studies the atmosphere (that's definitely high in the sky!) so they can make predictions about future weather events.

We are weather detectives!

So how do meteorologists predict the future? Do they use a crystal ball to tell them the forecast?

No, that would make it easier, but forecasting is less like predicting the future and more like solving a mystery. When a meteorologist forecasts the weather, they work like a weather detective. The more clues they have, the easier it is to find a solution, or in this case, the weather forecast.

An important part of forecasting is knowing what the weather is right now, not only for the surrounding area, but across the country and around the world. Why? Think of it this way, the Earth is covered with a blanket of air and that blanket is called the atmosphere. The air and water in the atmosphere and the water stored on Earth are constantly moving. This movement causes changes in the weather. The weather in another part of the country may be the weather where you are tomorrow.

Meteorologists take all the data they gather about the weather around the world and watch for patterns. Patterns often repeat themselves. Identifying these repeating patterns helps them make a more accurate forecast.

THE LAYERS OF EARTH'S ATMOSPHERE

MESOSPHERE
53 miles (85 km)

STRATOSPHERE
31 miles (50 km)

TROPOSPHERE
6.3 miles (10 km)

How do meteorologists use weather instruments to make a forecast? Do they form a band and play songs about the rain?

No, not those kinds of instruments! Meteorologists use weather instruments on the ground and in the sky to make their forecasts. These weather instruments measure temperature, wind, humidity, and barometric pressure. They also use satellites, Doppler radar, and Numerical Weather Prediction models.

WEATHER INSTRUMENTS & WHAT THEY DO

NAME	WHAT IT MEASURES
Thermometer	Temperature
Barometer	Atmospheric pressure
Anemometer	Wind speed and pressure
Weather vane	Wind direction
Rain gauge	Rainfall amounts

One of the most important instruments meteorologists use is called a radiosonde. It collects weather information, such as temperature, air pressure, relative humidity, and wind, and then sends a signal back to the weather station as it ascends into the sky.

weather satellite

Even higher than radiosondes are weather satellites. They monitor the Earth's weather from space. Satellite data shows meteorologists where clouds are and even where the strongest thunderstorms are located.

radiosonde

weather data

antenna

In the United States, most weather satellites are monitored by NOAA (the National Oceanic and Atmospheric Administration). NOAA monitors three types of weather satellites: geostationary satellites, polar orbiting satellites, and deep space satellites.

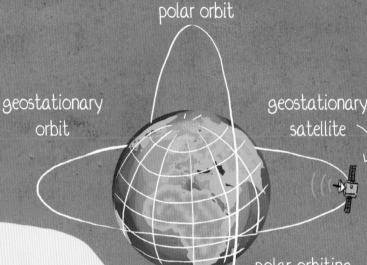

polar orbit

geostationary orbit

geostationary satellite

polar orbiting satellite

Geostationary satellites are located over 22,000 miles (35,405 km) above the Earth's equator and move at speeds almost as fast as the Earth's rotation. They take images of weather patterns and storms about every 30 seconds.

Polar orbiting satellites orbit the Earth north to south and pass by the Earth's poles. These satellites are about 500 miles (805 km) above the ground and orbit the Earth about 14 times each day. They collect a variety of data pertaining to the Earth's atmosphere and weather.

NOAA satellites gather data to learn more about our planet!

deep space satellite

1 million miles (1.6 million km)

The DSCOVR satellite is the only NOAA deep space satellite. It launched in 2015 and monitors solar winds and the weather conditions on Earth.

For information a little closer to the ground, meteorologists use something called ASOS, which stands for Automated Surface Observing Systems. They measure weather conditions on the Earth's surface.

These automated weather stations are located all around the world and help meteorologists know what is happening now on the ground. ASOS reports data about sky conditions, precipitation, temperature, barometric pressure, and wind up to 12 times an hour.

AUTOMATED SURFACE OBSERVING SYSTEMS (ASOS)

What ASOS Measures

- Cloud height and amount
  - Surface visibility
  - Rain, snow, and freezing rain intensity
  - Fog, haze, and dust
  - Sea-level pressure

- Air and dew point temperatures
  - Wind direction and speed
- Precipitation accumulation and more!

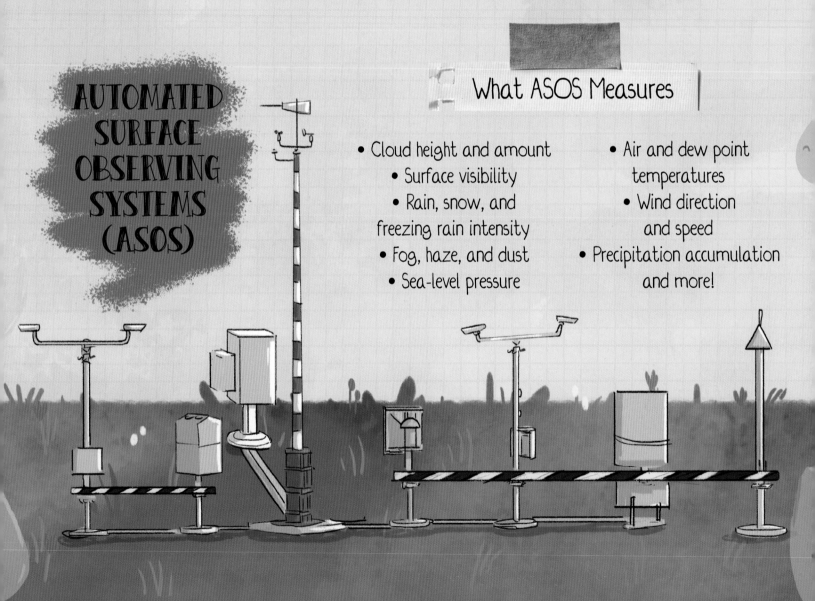

ASOS SITES

There are over 900 ASOS stations just in the United States.

That sure is A LOT of ASOS sites!

Meteorologists also use radars that are stationed on the ground. There are about 160 radar locations or sites across the United States operated by the National Weather Service and the military. Some television stations and private companies also operate radars. The type of radar they use is called a Doppler radar.

WEATHER RADAR

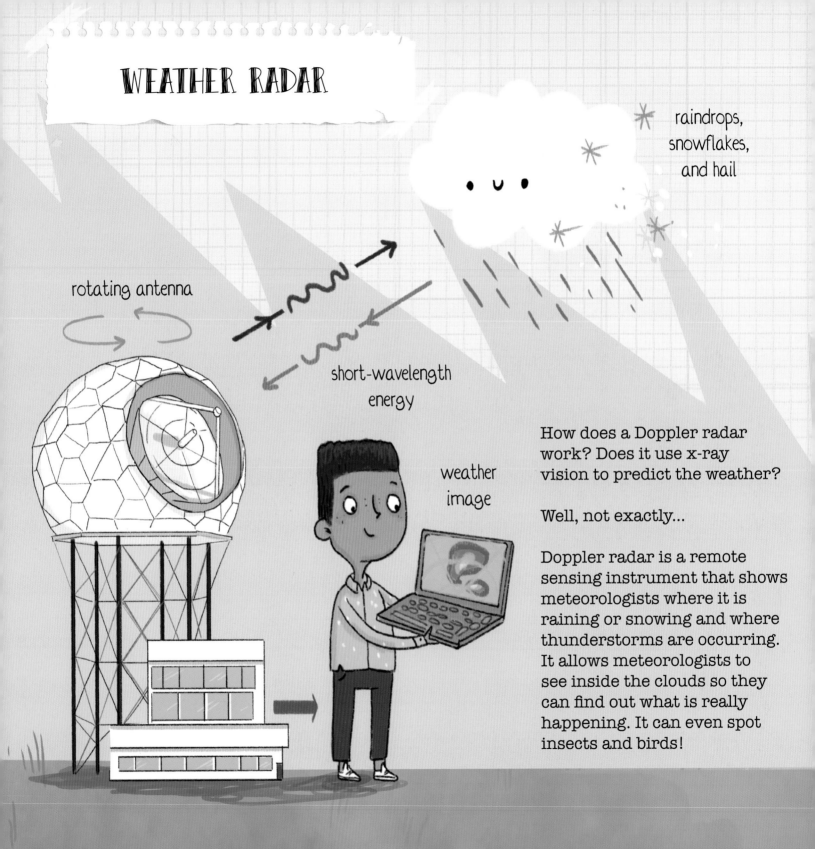

raindrops, snowflakes, and hail

rotating antenna

short-wavelength energy

weather image

How does a Doppler radar work? Does it use x-ray vision to predict the weather?

Well, not exactly...

Doppler radar is a remote sensing instrument that shows meteorologists where it is raining or snowing and where thunderstorms are occurring. It allows meteorologists to see inside the clouds so they can find out what is really happening. It can even spot insects and birds!

I'm Christian Hülsmeyer, the inventor of radar!

Radar stands for Radio Detection and Ranging. Strong radio waves are sent out by a transmitter. These waves hit objects in the distance (like a raindrop) and the waves come back. A receiver listens for the reflected waves and determines the different positions of objects. The change in frequency in the waves is called the Doppler effect. It can tell the precipitation size, amount, and speed within about a 100-mile (161 km) radius of the tower.

I'm Christian Doppler, the creator of the Doppler effect.

transmission frequency

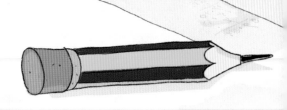

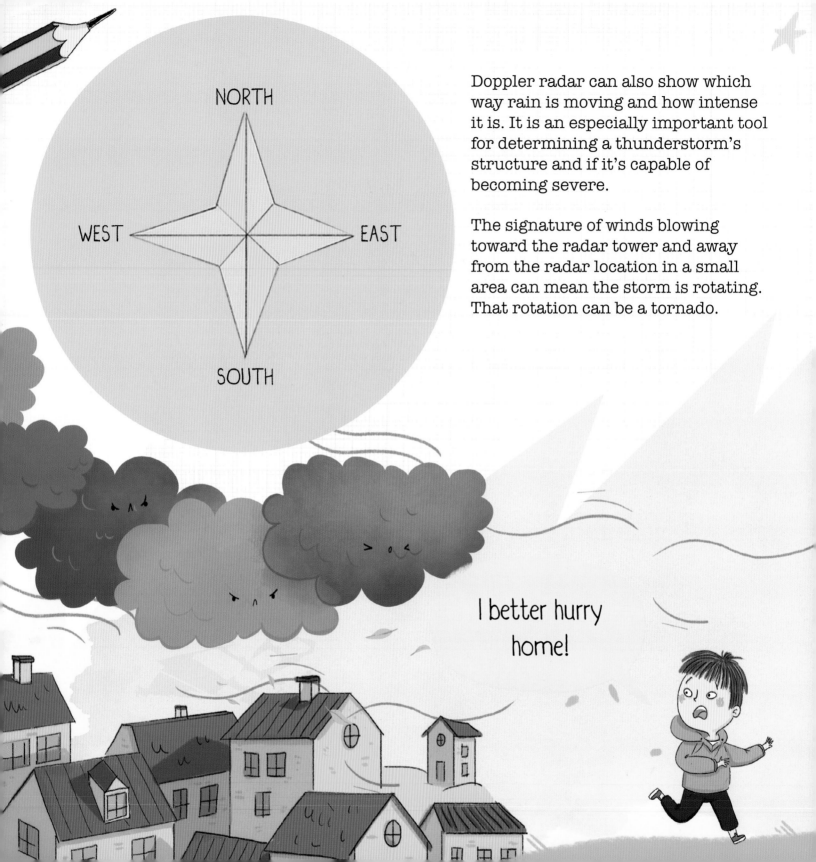

NORTH

WEST — EAST

SOUTH

Doppler radar can also show which way rain is moving and how intense it is. It is an especially important tool for determining a thunderstorm's structure and if it's capable of becoming severe.

The signature of winds blowing toward the radar tower and away from the radar location in a small area can mean the storm is rotating. That rotation can be a tornado.

I better hurry home!

If a storm is moving east at 30 mph (48 km/h) and it's currently 30 miles (48 km) to the west of you, it will arrive in one hour!

Meteorologists look for what appears as a "c" shape, or hook, on the radar image to locate a tornado. They also look at the winds. Red and green close together can also be a sign of a tornado.

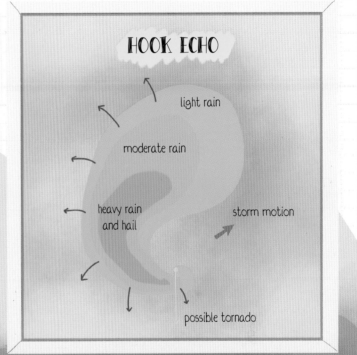

HOOK ECHO

light rain

moderate rain

heavy rain and hail

storm motion

possible tornado

A thunderstorm is considered severe if it can produce one or more of the following:

hail 1 inch (2.5 cm) in diameter or greater

winds that are 58 mph (93 km/h) or greater

tornado

How do weather balloons get into the sky? Do you just tie birthday balloons to weather equipment and send them high into the air?

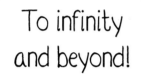

To infinity and beyond!

No, weather balloons aren't your average party balloons! They are much bigger and much thicker. Weather balloons are made of latex or neoprene and are 6 feet (2 m) in diameter. They can grow up to 20 feet (6 m) as they rise!

Weather balloons are launched twice a day every day of the year from over 900 locations across the world. About 100 are launched in the United States and the US territories by the National Weather Service. The balloon flight lasts about two hours and rises to over 100,000 feet (30 km).

WEATHER BALLOONS

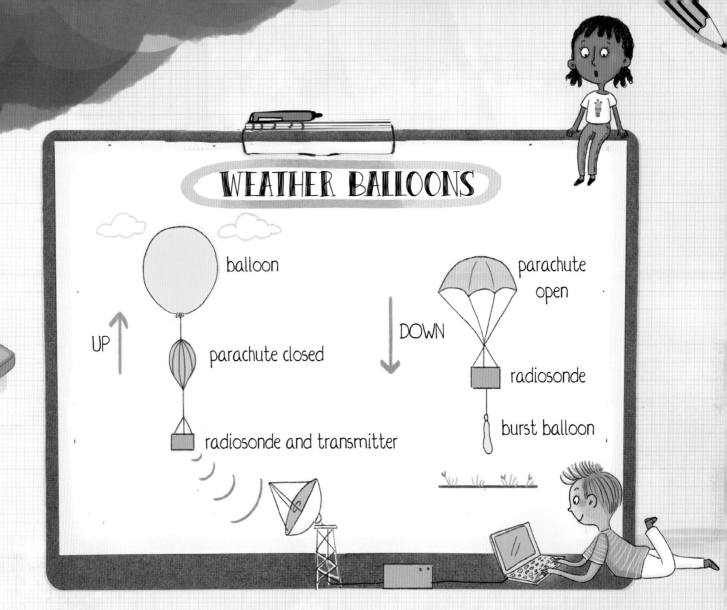

balloon

UP

parachute closed

radiosonde and transmitter

DOWN

parachute open

radiosonde

burst balloon

Each balloon is equipped with a battery powered radiosonde, a transmitter, and a parachute. As the balloon goes up, the weather instruments in the radiosonde record the temperature, relative humidity, and air pressure. Every one to two seconds the transmitter sends the information back to a tracking device. By tracking the position of the balloon, the wind speed and direction can also be calculated.

The weather balloon and radiosonde endure extreme weather conditions as they ascend, from frigid cold temperatures to very high wind and extremely low air pressure. Because of these conditions and the way the balloon is made, it will eventually burst. When it does, the parachute brings it gently back to Earth at a speed of under 22 miles per hour (35 km/h).

A weather balloon?!?!?!

Thank you!

FUN FACT

All radiosondes come with a mailing bag and instructions on what to do if you find one. If a radiosonde is returned, it is fixed so it can be reused!

Weather balloons are very valuable tools because radiosondes are the main source of weather data above the ground. The data is used in Numerical Weather Prediction models, research, and local storm forecasts. Without this information, accurate forecasts beyond a few hours would be nearly impossible!

Looks like we'll have sun all week!

That's great!

How do meteorologists use all the data they have collected to create a forecast? Do they store it in a really big library somewhere up in space and never look at it again?

It is a lot of information to go through, but they do go through it! Most meteorologists find it helpful to look at the weather data plotted on a map or charts so they can see how the weather is moving across the country.

For example, if there is cold air across the midwestern part of the United States, they can determine where the cold air is moving next. You may see this represented on a map as a blue line with triangles. This is called a cold front and the triangles show the direction the cold air is moving. If there is warm air across the southeastern United States, then they can identify where it is going. On the map, a red line would mark the warm front and half circles would show which way it's headed.

But remember it's not just about what's happening at ground level, it's also about what's happening in the layers above the surface several miles up. The temperature, moisture, wind speed, and wind direction change the higher up you go.

Meteorologists use their scientific knowledge of the atmosphere and their experience to see these patterns to predict the weather, but they also use math. That's right—math!

My beach day is ruined!

Sorry, man! I didn't have enough data!

Numerical Weather Prediction (NWP) models are computer models that solve complex sets of mathematical equations based on the physical properties of the atmosphere. The equations use all the data collected from the weather instruments you just learned about, such as current observations of temperature, air pressure, wind speed, humidity, and water levels, to analyze and predict the weather.

Supercomputers process several NWP models multiple times a day. These models can simulate the weather on maps of the surface and various other layers of the atmosphere to give a meteorologist a visual snapshot of what the weather may look like on a particular day at a particular time. The models can provide forecasts days in advance! The tricky part is that there are numerous models and they don't always agree. That's where a meteorologist's experience, math skills, and scientific knowledge come in handy!

The weather forecast was correct!

What a beautiful sunny day!

How do broadcast meteorologists know what to say when they are talking about the weather on TV? Does a little bird sit on their shoulder and tell them what to say?

No way! Before the news, meteorologists spend time researching the weather of the day using clues from all the tools you learned about to make their forecast. This would be similar to you doing research before giving a presentation to your class.

Local Weather

The meteorologist will then prepare maps, charts, and illustrations on a special weather graphics computer to show during the newscast. Once it is time to present the weather, meteorologists will gather their graphics and step in front of the green screen. The green screen will show viewers the graphics they made on their TV.

Oops!

News stations use green screens to allow broadcast meteorologists to present the weather to viewers! The meteorologist stands in front of a green background and a chroma key filter is added to the screen so that viewers can see a map on their device even though the background remains green. Anything green is changed by the chroma filter!

Unlike news anchors who read a script from a teleprompter, meteorologists adlib the weathercasts. Most meteorologists use their graphics as an outline as they are talking. (This takes a lot of practice!)

A lot of work goes into predicting the weather. As you can see, it is like solving a mystery with the meteorologist looking for all the right clues. When you put it all together, we can be prepared for any kind of weather!

MEET BROADCAST METEOROLOGIST LISA SPENCER

Lisa Spencer is a long-time broadcast meteorologist at WSMV in Nashville, Tennessee. She shares her passion for weather and weather safety with community groups and school children, speaking to hundreds of students each year. Lisa earned a master's degree in geography with a concentration in atmospheric science from the University of Memphis as well as a bachelor's degree in broadcast communications. Lisa has been recognized nationally by the American Meteorological Society and The National Weather Association. She is also the author of this book!

Here is Lisa in front of a green screen telling viewers about the weather!

Q: What do you love most about being a meteorologist?

L.S.: My favorite thing about being a meteorologist is teaching people how to be prepared for severe storms like tornadoes and hurricanes. Whether it's on TV or visiting a school, I enjoy sharing what I know about the weather.

MAKE YOUR OWN THUNDERSTORM

Become a meteorologist at home and watch as a storm forms before your eyes!

What you need:

- Ice cube tray
- Food coloring (red and blue)
- Clear plastic container (roughly the size of a dinner plate)

Directions:

1. Fill the ice cube tray with water.
2. Carefully put a few drops of blue food coloring in each slot and mix. Then place the tray in the freezer for 4 hours or until frozen.
3. After the ice cubes have frozen, fill the clear plastic container with water. Be sure the water is room temperature and the container is about 3/4 full.
4. At the same time, drop 3 or 4 drops of red food coloring into the left side of the container and place 4 blue ice cubes into the right side of the container.

Discussion:

What happened when you dropped the ice into the container?
Why did the blue food coloring sink? What happened to the red food coloring?

Science behind storms:

Watch how the blue ice cubes begin to sink and melt. As the colors begin to move toward each other, the colder blue water pushes the room temperature water up. This is a lot like how a storm forms. Cold air forces warmer air up into the sky where it will condense into clouds that become thunderstorms!

MAKE YOUR OWN WEATHER VANE

Meteorologists use lots of instruments to predict big weather events including tornadoes. Try making your very own weather instrument at home!

What you need:

- Compass
- Markers or crayons
- 12" x 12" square piece of cardboard
- Scissors
- Paper straw
- Construction paper
- Sharpened pencil
- Pin
- Clay

Directions:

1. Use your compass to find north. Once you know which way is north, label your cardboard with the directions (north, east, south, and west). North is at the top and south is on the bottom. East is always to the right of north and west is always to the left. Feel free to decorate the remaining parts of the cardboard however you like!

2. Carefully cut a small slit on each end of the straw (about half an inch (1.27 cm)).

3. Draw an arrow and a tail (a pentagon shape is easiest for the tail) on a piece of construction paper. Then carefully cut out both pieces.

4. Place the arrow in the slit on one end of the straw and the tail in the slit on the other end of the straw.

5. Roll a fist-sized ball of clay into a circle and place it in the center of your labeled cardboard. Then carefully stick the sharpened side of the pencil into the clay so it is sticking straight up.

6. Very carefully use the pin to secure the straw to the pencil eraser. Center the straw over the pencil horizontally and place the pin directly through the straw and into the eraser. Wiggle the straw a little bit so that it can spin more easily.

7. Set your weather vane outside and observe which way the arrow points!

Discussion:

Which way was the arrow pointing once you set your weather vane down? What does that tell you about the wind? Why would it be helpful for meteorologists to know which way the wind is blowing?

Here is a weather vane you might see in your town!

GLOSSARY

Air pressure – the weight of the air that is above the Earth's surface

Anemometer – a weather instrument used for determining wind speed and pressure

ASOS – (Automated Surface Observing Systems) data reporting group that measures temperature, barometric pressure, and wind

Atmosphere – the gases around the Earth where weather takes place

Barometer – a weather instrument that measures changes in atmospheric pressure

Broadcast meteorologist – a meteorologist who relays information about the weather on TV

Climate – the average weather for an area after several years

Cold front – when warm air is replaced by cold air in our atmosphere

Doppler radar – a weather instrument that determines wind direction, wind speed, precipitation, and more

Forecasting – an educated guess made by meteorologists about weather conditions based on information collected from weather instruments

Geostationary orbit – the route that geostationary satellites take as they move along the Earth's equator

Polar orbit – the route that polar satellites take moving north to south

Radar – a system that uses energy in the form of waves to sense objects, such as rain

Radiosonde – a weather instrument attached to a balloon that can measure humidity and temperature

Weather graphics – maps and other images that display data collected by meteorologists when reporting the weather

Weather satellites – satellites that orbit Earth and monitor the weather

Weather vane – a weather instrument that measures the direction of the wind

Wind speed – the speed of air moving from one area to another